CENTRAL ELEMENTARY
SCHOOL

SHARKS

NURSE SHARKS

JOHN F. PREVOST
ABDO & Daughters

Published by Abdo & Daughters, 4940 Viking Drive, Suite 622, Edina, Minnesota 55435.

Library bound edition distributed by Rockbottom Books, Pentagon Tower, P.O. Box 36036, Minneapolis, Minnesota 55435.

Printed in the United States.

Cover Photo credit: Peter Arnold, Inc.
Interior Photo credits: Peter Arnold, Inc.

Edited by Bob Italia

Library of Congress Cataloging-in-Publication

Prevost, John F.
    Nurse sharks / by John F. Prevost.
        p.   cm. — (Sharks)
Includes bibliographical references and index.
ISBN 1-56239-472-X
1. Nurse shark—Juvenile literature. 2. Ginglymostomatidae —Juvenile
literature. [1. Nurse shark. 2. Sharks.]   I. Title.
II . Series: Prevost, John F. Sharks.
QL638.95.G55P74   1995
597'.31—dc20   95-1173
                                                                      CIP
                                                                      AC

ABOUT THE AUTHOR
    John Prevost is a marine biologist and diver who has been active in conservation and education issues for the past 18 years. Currently he is living inland and remains actively involved in freshwater and marine husbandry, conservation and education projects.

Contents

NURSE SHARKS AND FAMILY

Sharks are fish without **scales**. A rough covering of **denticles** protects their skin. Sharks do not have a bony skeleton. Their skeleton is made of **cartilage**, a tough, stretchy tissue.

There are 3 different nurse sharks: short-tail, tawny nurse, and nurse. They live in **tropical** and **sub-tropical** oceans.

Nurse sharks are sometimes found in groups, resting one on top of the other on the ocean bottom. Once, scientists believed that nurse sharks protected their young and nursed them. Now we know they only clump together when resting. Because of this behavior, they were named "nurse" sharks. Related sharks are the wobbegongs and zebra sharks.

Nurse sharks often rest on the ocean bottom.

WHAT THEY LOOK LIKE

Nurse sharks are thick-bodied with wide heads. The short-tail nurse shark is the smallest and only grows up to 30 inches (75 cm) long. The largest nurse shark **species** may grow up to 14 feet (4.3 meters) long. The females of all 3 nurse shark species are larger than the males.

Nurse sharks have 2 **barbels**. These are pointed lumps of skin in front of the mouth. They help the shark taste and touch objects to find food.

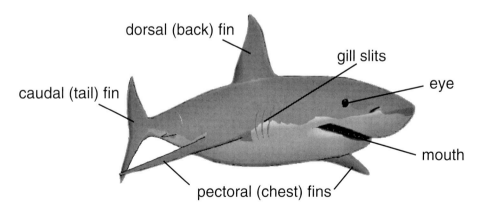

dorsal (back) fin

gill slits

eye

caudal (tail) fin

mouth

pectoral (chest) fins

Most sharks share the same features.

A nurse shark is thick-bodied with a wide head.
It has 2 barbels in front of its mouth.

Nurse sharks are brown or tan. The young sharks are marked with dark spots on their backs. Nurse sharks are slow swimmers. They like to hunt along the ocean bottom at night.

WHERE THEY LIVE

Nurse sharks are found close to shore in **tropical** and **sub-tropical** ocean waters. They live in **coral reefs**, **lagoons**, and even in sandy surf areas.

Nurse sharks often hunt in shallow water. But they have been found in water as deep as 230 feet (70 meters).

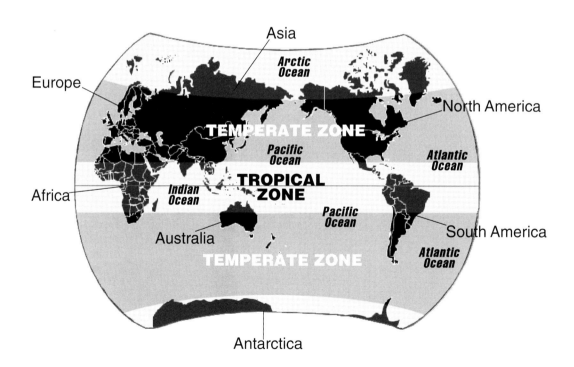

Nurse sharks live in shallow water where predators cannot reach them.

Nurse sharks are sluggish during the day. They are often found in **schools** of 3 or more, resting against or on top of each other. They will return to the same daytime resting places after their nightly feeding.

FOOD

All sharks are **predators**. They eat other animals. Since nurse sharks are not fast swimmers, they eat slow-moving or sleeping **prey**. These sharks will swim slowly over the ocean bottom and suck prey out of sand, gravel, or **coral**.

Nurse sharks eat **mollusks**, **sea urchins**, small shellfish and fish. Even fast-swimming coral **reef** fish will become food if the nurse shark catches them sleeping.

Young nurse sharks often rest on the ocean bottom with their heads raised. Scientists believe this is a way of surprising prey that uses the underside of the shark for shelter.

Nurse sharks swim slowly over the bottom and suck prey out of sand, gravel, or coral.

SENSES

Nurse sharks do not have good eyesight. But they do have good senses of taste and smell. They will swim along the bottom with their **barbels** barely touching the surface. Sense organs cover the barbels and much of the shark's skin.

Sharks can sense the **electric field** of hidden **prey**. All animals with nervous systems give off a weak electric field. The nurse shark's skill to sense this field allows it to find prey below sand or in **coral reefs**.

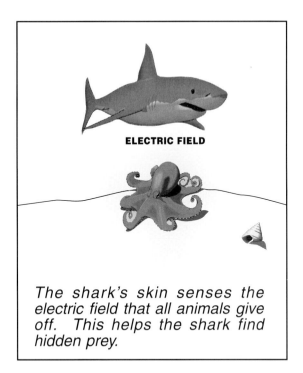

ELECTRIC FIELD

The shark's skin senses the electric field that all animals give off. This helps the shark find hidden prey.

Nurse sharks use their barbels to feel their way along the ocean bottom. Their eyesight is poor.

BABIES

Newborn nurse sharks are called pups. A **litter** is 4 to 30 pups. Some nurse shark species hatch their young from eggs outside the mother. Most nurse shark pups hatch inside their mother and are fed by a **yolk sac**.

The young nurse sharks are 10 to 16 inches (27 to 40 cm) long at birth. The nurse shark pups are marked with dark spots that fade as the sharks grow.

The egg case of a nurse shark. It contains the unhatched eggs.

ATTACK AND DEFENSE

Nurse sharks have small mouths and strong jaws. Their teeth are made for gripping **prey** and not for cutting. They have 22 to 38 teeth per row. These teeth are arranged so more than one row is in use at a time. This gives the nurse shark a better gripping and crushing surface. When teeth are lost or damaged, new teeth will move up from rows of teeth behind the working teeth.

A large nurse shark has almost nothing to fear except man. Nurse sharks live in shallow water, where many **predators** cannot reach them. Larger fish and other nurse sharks prey on smaller nurse sharks.

The shark pups blend in with their surroundings and are hard to see. They are also very still in the daytime. As they grow older, these sharks group together when at rest.

Nurse sharks are often found in schools of 3 or more resting against each other.

Scientists believe this grouping protects nurse sharks from enemies. When attacked, the group will scatter. This makes it hard for the **predator** to chase them.

ATTACKS ON HUMANS

Nurse sharks are found in warm, shallow ocean waters—where people like to swim and play. Contact between humans and nurse sharks happens often. Nurse sharks are dangerous only when bothered.

There have been many reports of sharks biting or bumping into people who bother them. There are no known human deaths from nurse shark attacks.

The nurse shark.

GLOSSARY

Barbels: A slender lump of skin used to sense odors and taste in water.

Cartilage (CAR-tuh-lij): A firm and stretchy tissue, like gristle.

Coral: A hard substance resembling limestone, usually found in tropical waters.

Denticle (DEN-tih-kull): A small tooth-like structure that protects a shark's skin and makes it rough to the touch.

Electric field: An electric-charged area surrounding an animal's body, created by the nervous system.

Gill slits: A part of the body of a fish by which it gets oxygen from water.

Lagoon: A shallow body of water partly cut off from the sea by a narrow strip of land.

Litter: Young animals born at one time.

Mollusk: A group of animals (clams, oysters, and snails) typically covered by a hard outer covering or shell.

Predator (PRED-uh-tor): An animal that hunts and eats other animals.

Prey: An animal that is hunted for food.

Reef: A narrow ridge of coral at or near the water surface.

Scales: Platelike structures forming all or part of the outer covering of certain animals, such as snakes and fish.

Schools: A large group of fish or water animals of the same kind swimming together.

Sea urchins: Any of a group of sea animals having a shell covered with hard, movable spines.

Species: A group of related living things that shares basic characteristics.
Sub-tropical (sub-TRAH-pih-kull): Regions bordering on the tropics; having a nearly tropical climate.
Tropical (TRAH-pih-kull): The part of the Earth's surface lying between the Tropic of Cancer (23.5 degrees north) and the Tropic of Capricorn (23.5 degrees south).
Yolk sac: A pouch containing a food substance for the unborn sharks.

BIBLIOGRAPHY

Budker, Paul. *The Life of Sharks*. London: Weidenfeld and Nicolson, 1971.

Compagno, Leonard. FAO Species Catalogue Vol. 4, *Sharks of the World.* United Nations Development Programme, Rome, 1984.

Gilbert, P. W., ed. *Sharks, Skates, and Rays*. Maryland: Johns Hopkins Press, 1967.

Macquitty, Miranda. *Shark*. New York: Alfred A. Knopf, 1992.

Sattler, Helen. *Sharks, the Super Fish*. New York: Lothrop, Lee & Shepard Books, 1986.

Server, Lee. *Sharks*. New York City: Gallery Books, 1990.

Index